Lockdown
Lawyers
D0413078

Editors

Emma Trevett is a paralegal in the public law and human rights team at Irwin Mitchell LLP. She has worked at Bristol Law Centre since 2013. Emma is part of the Young Legal Aid Lawyers (YLAL) national committee. She received a special mention in The Amnesty International Brave Awards 2020 for her human rights work. Emma has recently been exempted from the training contract by the SRA and is looking forward to a long career in legal aid. Her poetry can be found on social media under @etpoetrybank.

Jon Whitfield QC was called to the bar in 1985 and took silk in 2010. He defends in cases of homicide, terrorism and fraud, advises in regulatory proceedings and sits as a judge in Mental Health Tribunals and the Court of Protection. This is set against a love of nature, observing, photographing and writing about those small occurrences that would otherwise go unnoticed. He is a trustee of Winchester Poetry Festival. His poetry, photography and books can be found at www.jonwynne.co.uk.

The purpose of Legal Action Group is to promote equal access to justice for all members of society who are socially, economically or otherwise disadvantaged. To this end, it seeks to improve law and practice, the administration of justice and legal services.

Edited by Emma Trevett
and Jon Whitfield QC

Legal Action Group
2020

This edition published in Great Britain 2020
by LAG Education and Service Trust Limited
National Pro Bono Centre, 48 Chancery Lane, London WC2A 1JF

www.lag.org.uk

British Library Cataloguing in Publication Data

A CIP catalogue record for this book is available from the British Library.

This book has been produced using Forest Stewardship Council (FSC) certified paper. The wood used to produce FSC certified products with a 'Mixed Sources' label comes from FSC certified well-managed forests, controlled sources and/or recycled material.

ISBN 978 1 913648 00 8

Typeset by RefineCatch Limited, Bungay, Suffolk
Printed in Great Britain by Hobbs the Printers, Totton, Hampshire

Foreword

Jon Whitfield QC, Doughty Street Chambers

I am delighted to introduce this collection of poetry written by and dedicated to that much maligned group of people, legal aid lawyers, together with their long-suffering families and their clients. When Emma asked if I would write something for a collection to mark the effect of COVID-19 on the legal aid system, I immediately thought it was a brilliant idea. I expected some gentle support from colleagues, a few smiles and 'oh yes, that's nice'. Neither of us imagined there would be such an overwhelmingly positive response both in the number and quality of contributions and in the support from friends and colleagues.

The original brief to writers was deceptively simple: write about how you see the current lockdown and near collapse of the legal system. How have you coped? Have you coped!? How has your family coped? What are your pathways for the future? How have you continued to support clients? The result has been everything from haiku to lengthy poems covering falling revenue, falling ceilings, the fear of infection in dirty courts, police stations and prisons with no PPE, the despair of clients in custody or facing huge challenges with cases postponed indefinitely. There are poems about video hearings, children and home-schooling, paying a mortgage or retaining staff when you find you have no income and little/no support from government. In short, all the old worries are present despite the legal lockdown. They have just increased hugely.

My initial thoughts for this introduction revolved around those last points: how has the publicly funded legal system survived this pandemic at all, given it has endured 35 years of cuts whilst saddled with huge increases in expense and workload? However, as I pondered and read the contributions, I realised the answer is simple. It is the lawyers that work themselves to a standstill to keep a broken system going. Suffering physical and mental ill-health and worse, whether by COVID-19 or any number of difficulties. It is their families and the chambers and firms that continue to support them in their work. It is the ability of these same practitioners and their families to smile and joke and, despite all the pressures they face, to take a deep breath and carry on.

Here then is the impact of COVID-19 on everyday legal aid lawyers and the system they prop-up against all the odds. The worries and the wants, the tears and smiles and, the determination to do a job well, against seemingly insurmountable obstacles. The genesis of this book may be the current storm, but it stands as testament to those people who are weathering it. I hope you enjoy it as much as I have.

Jon Whitfield QC
Hampshire
May 2020

Preface

Writing poetry and practicing law may seem to be an unusual combination at first. However, over the years I have found the two to be complimentary. The ability to think creatively helps to resolve legal issues. The experiences I have had in law have developed my understanding of others and myself in some respects.

I have been writing poetry for as long as I can remember. I share my poetry on social media and I often attend open-mic nights in Bristol. I am regularly featured on BBC Radio Bristol and was the first performer for the national launch of BBC Upload's virtual open-mic night.

We do things as children without fear. We write, paint and play music but we sometimes lose touch with that as adults which is sad. My motivation for sharing poetry more widely is to encourage more people to write. I believe that everyone has something unique to say which is beautiful and clearly demonstrated within this collection.

I am part of the national committee of Young Legal Aid Lawyers (YLAL). We are a group of lawyers committed to practising in areas of law that have traditionally been publicly funded. We campaign for a sustainable legal aid system, promote the interests of junior lawyers and provide a network for people beginning their careers in legal aid work. From the onset of the COVID-19 pandemic we turned our attention to running virtual events. A tradition soon developed of reading a poem after these events.

It was after attending one of these events that I formed the idea for *Lockdown Lawyers*. I sent out a message on Twitter calling for anonymous poetry from legal aid lawyers. I was astounded by the response! Poems flooded in from around the country. I was surprised to find other lawyers that regularly wrote poetry and, that those who did not were excited to have a go. The fact the poems were anonymous allowed the writers to express themselves freely. The quality of the poems I received was outstanding and touched on many important issues affecting lawyers in lockdown.

YLAL's COVID-19 Report dated April 2020 found that 67.5 per cent of members stated their work had decreased, significantly decreased or had been decimated by the crisis. One barrister stated that COVID-19 was having a devastating financial impact and their income had completely stopped overnight. The survey found that 18.2 per cent of members were still required to attend court and 25 per cent were required to put themselves at risk of infection by attending police stations or conducting face-to-face meetings.

These are challenging times for the legal aid sector which makes projects like *Lockdown Lawyers* essential to raise both funds and awareness. It is also an opportunity to create something positive and remarkable during these unprecedented times. I hope that this book will make legal aid lawyers feel united in a time where we are physically apart.

The proceeds of this book will go the Law Centres Network. Law Centres provide legal advice and representation to those who otherwise would be unable to afford a lawyer. They operate on a not-for-profit basis and I hope that that the money raised from this book will enable them to help more people.

This anthology of poems relies on the contributions of others. First, I would like to thank all the legal aid lawyers that contributed such thoughtful and insightful poems. I would also like to thank my colleagues over the years who have worked tirelessly for vulnerable clients and provided me with endless inspiration. My thanks also go to Jon Whitfield QC who was instrumental in making this project a reality. I would also like to thank David Gardner for the cover image. Finally, I would like to thank the publisher, Esther Pilger, and Legal Action Group who are committed to improving access to justice.

I would also like to send my personal thanks to all NHS staff during this difficult time. I would like to thank Ward 6 of Leighton Hospital who cared for my granddad Brian Anderton who sadly passed away during the pandemic.

Emma Trevett
Bristol
May 2020

Contributors

Adam Griffiths	Queen Square Chambers
Ana Potter	Autism campaigner
Audrey Ludwig	Suffolk Law Centre
Becky Kingi	Anti-Trafficking and Labour Exploitation Unit (ATLEU)
Bethany Parr	Irwin Mitchell LLP
Callum Slade	Son of Claire Slade, Irwin Mitchell LLP
Carl Buckley	Guernica 37
Charlie Sherrard QC	Furnival Chambers
Colin Monehen	Foxes Solicitors
CrimeGirl	Twitter
David Maunder	Queen Square Chambers
David Richards	3 Paper Buildings
David York	Irwin Mitchell LLP
Dominik Morton	Queen Square Chambers
Emma Trevett	Irwin Mitchell LLP
Emma Waldron	3 Paper Buildings
Greg Ó Ceallaigh	Garden Court Chambers
Greg Powell	Powell Spencer and Partners
Gregory Gordon	Guildhall Chambers
Jack Duffy	Queen Square Chambers
Jack Tebbutt	Son of Emma Howes, Irwin Mitchell LLP
Jake Davey	Partner of Polly Sweeney, Rook Irwin Sweeney LLP
Jeinsen Lam	South West London Law Centre
Jess Street	Queen Square Chambers
Jessica Habel	Pallant Chambers
Jon Whitfield QC	Doughty Street Chambers
Jonathan Mole	9 King's Bench Walk
Josie Hicklin	Greater Manchester Law Centre
Karen Bowers	Bristol Law Centre
Kate Bex QC	Red Lion Chambers
Katie Wilson	Serjeants' Inn Chambers
Katy Moulton	Irwin Mitchell LLP

Keima Payton	Payton's Solicitors
Kriti Upadhyay	Guildhall Chambers
Lee Davies	Goldstones Solicitors
Lucy Reed	St John's Chambers
Malvika Jaganmohan	St Ives Chambers
Mandy Groves	Ealing Law Centre
Maximilian Hardy	9 Bedford Row
Michael Etienne	No 5 Chambers
Michael Stokes QC	Former Recorder of Nottingham
Oliver Kirk	Five St Andrew's Hill
Pamela Rose	1MCB
Paul Storey QC	29 Bedford Row
Remy Mohamed	Grenfell Inquiry Coordination Officer
Renee Southern	Broudie Jackson Canter
Richard Wright QC	Park Square Barristers
Russell Conway	Oliver Fisher Solicitors
Ruth Armstrong	Queen Square Chambers
Secret Barrister	Secret Barrister HQ
Sian Pearce	Bristol Law Centre
Sophie Earnshaw	Shelter
Thomas Cole	Queen Square Chambers
Tony Clear	Father-in-law of Alex Ruck Keene, 39 Essex Chambers
Wendy Pettifer	Anti-Trafficking and Labour Exploitation Unit (ATLEU)

A Crisis for Joe Public

In times forgotten now retold anew,
a plague does spread and kill without a sue.
The law doth change, courts sit sans retinue
and all the while exotic mews bray through.

The people clap yet fear for their own kind;
silent death spreads wheezing all the time.
Of deaths untold in care homes and online;
a tiger's jaws grip tighter than headlines.

At first quiet resolve from daily toil
but then the tedium of mortal spoil.
The lines do move, exponent and derived
but none can tell just who this week survives.

And all the while exotic mews bray through.

They shall grow...?

On ANZAC day we remember them not?

They, fallen like new mown unsaleable poppies.
The one hundred and ninety thousand, nine hundred and eighty-five
of Johns Hopkins' scientifically sombre website.
In today's ticking tally,
shall have grown old
or sick,
or euphemistically
designated, among those
with pre-existing conditions.
Like me, 'immunocompromised'.
The random young,
or those who selflessly care for them
with varying or limited protections...
Dispensable...
Like the cannon fodder of earlier wars
The low paid, insecurely working hard
rounding up shopping trolleys, disinfecting.
Indispensable...?

When too many of our leaders
of the 'free world',
Incompetently
watch the markets in free fall
and panic at loss of favour,
in fear of missing out on re-election.

The fall of Rome
Repeated?
As Neros fiddle
And Pontius Pilate washes his hands
The scientists are ignored or sacked
by men
who should be grown-ups.

A ray of hope
The women leaders of our world
Seemingly better at the calculus
of preserving lives versus livelihoods

While our gossip and quackery magnifying platforms
pretend not to be publishers
as arm's length algorithms rake it in,
and corporately tainted
pseudo-economists, commentators
political overseers
calculate the value of
the freedom to sit in a café or
queue for a burger or a game
in a premature return
to a false normalcy.
While in a calculated risk
to gain safety for the 'deemed at risk'
the old may stay
Sequestered indoors, indeed
At the going down of the sun and in the morning.

Will we remember them?

The C-19 Law Centre

I stare at the square
The rectangle of light in the corner of the spare room.
Hour after hour
Words, a quick clip, more words.
And the Zoom and the Teams, the oversized pixilation
Familiar faces with unfamiliar backdrops, domestic, blurry, fantastical
Me, struggling to lip read as the images flutter
in and out,
Lips moving but sound comes later.
Work, play, more Zoom, more Teams
punctuated by questioning emails.
Can you help me? Can you help me?
Can you help me?
The emailer, stuck in their problem
stuck in a different room,
Their written plea a ransom request.
I want to see them, shake their hand, comfort them
let them see me
I do what I can, I am with you and for you
computer shall not say 'no', in my spare room.

I wish I had a bookcase

I need to get a bookcase for the background of my Zoom
I need to get a bookcase for an intellectual room

I can't appear in court with this background that I've got
That washing horse is far too close the Judge will see the lot

He'll see the kids' pyjamas he'll see the Mrs' bra
I wonder if I'd fit a bookcase in the back of my small car

I'll just have to move the washing to the corner of the room
I better put the suit on the Mags will connect quite soon

It's too hot for the whistle these shorts will do just fine
They'll only see the top half I'm sure it's nearly time

Before the bench in flip flops whoever would have thought
But what if they ask you to stand up plug out last resort

I hope the kids don't come in as I'm pleading here for bail
He really has got asthma Sir no place for him is gaol

I look a proper nana here upon my chair
Shirt jacket tie and flip flops and homemade haircut hair

I wish I had a bookcase for the background in this room
I hope this bloody lockdown ends at some point soon

Telephone

I sit quietly at my desk as
the telephone screams at me.
It screams and, screams again.
And they are desperate screams.
These are the screams of clients.
They will not go away nor can they as
there are few of us to scream at.
Later I dream of those screams of desperate people,
but I do not see their faces just hear their agony.
The dream turns to a nightmare as I torment myself
thinking about their despair.
But I cannot wake, and I am engulfed in forms to fill and
the never-ending ring tone of a Legal Aid Office.
Now it is me screaming at the phone.
But I wake.
It is another day and
the telephones start to scream at me.

Distant Light

The night skies are clearer now
And the smog is ebbing away
The stars are finding their way back through
Like the days of navigating from the prow.

We don't really see the stars
Only their memories,
Light that is beyond old
In the time it took to travel so far.

If you look when it is dark
Just think of what that means
And what might have passed,
Things don't ever remain stark.

Before & After – A locked down lawyer

0930
Arrive at court, damn, I'm on last.
But daddy, spaghetti IS breakfast.

1030
The Crown contends failure to surrender.
No, I just said, DON'T put your hand in the blender.

1130
Let's look at your statement, page three.
You can watch Frozen but only 'til tea.

1230
Then he broke into the house, it was pitch dark.
Right, that's it! We're going to the park.

1330
Can you dash to Pret? I'll have the smoked salmon.
What do you mean yucky? You always have the ham one.

1430
And sure means sure, beyond reasonable doubt.
No, we can't go again, we've already been out.

1530
Yes, I promise I'll get home to see the children.
One day I'll be back in court again.

COVID Limerick No 5

It's all very well to do Zoom,
but it's better to be in the room.
One misses the 'tells',
the ticks and the smells,
there's a danger injustice will loom!

The Fight Continues

When lockdown came
The world was unsure
What to do next
And how to endure

The hospitals busy
The care home doors closed
No court hearings in person
More restrictions imposed

Clients were fearful
Their families too
Already dealing with so much
Not sure what else they could do

How to protect relatives
When you can't visit their care home?
And how to protect yourself
When you're left on your own?

To the legal aid lawyers
It was without doubt
They must continue their fight
And ride this storm out

The offices closed
Lawyers working from home
Training on video
And meetings by phone

New guidance daily
New legislation too
For the legal aid lawyers
So much was new

But legal aid lawyers
Never give up the fight
For they know the importance
Of standing up for what's right

The question of court hearings
How they would remotely proceed
Was one that legal aid lawyers
Were unsure would succeed

But ideas quickly shared
And best practice discussed
Court hearings continued
Everyone worked hard to adjust

The legal aid lawyers
Know now it is key
To work even harder
To protect those in need

The lockdown is difficult
We too struggle some days
But we push on to help our clients
Through this difficult phase

We may be in lockdown
We may be apart
But the legal aid lawyers
Have been here from the start

We don't give up hope
We don't give up the fight
For as long as our client's need us
We'll be standing up for their rights.

In Limbo

People who break the law
Don't obey government guidance
Dirty Courts
People congregating in waiting areas
No social distancing

Barristers who live and breathe their work
Miss it terribly
But are frightened to go back to it
Because living and breathing it
Could mean dying from it

We live in a world on two different axles

just when you thought you had a grip on the world
it evaporates into the 10 o'clock news;
into broken thrones & dusty faces,
less swaying hips,
less dropping hints.
(forever is on its way but I guess it's taking the long route)

and so sometimes all there is to do is listen, get deep
into that 'pay attention to how things blend, honey'
opening-up:
vulnerable: with all that knees folded and hands clasped
brilliance smeared all over your face
messing your perfect, your privilege, your everything
right up.
and though it burns, risk delight
trip over yourself
and kiss.
gulp down that ruach soul: get to know your Arabic, your heart bends,
you're holy,
& let yourself get up to something

(why is this not see through? not always made of ribbons and dancing.
-lament-
grazed knees on the carpet.
reimagine, grip tight, drip grace:

though this moment tastes of grit
a new world is on the way

Walk to Work

I can no longer stroke the warm, worn stonework
On my walk to work through St John's churchyard.
Once Loddiges market gardens of rhubarb and rhododendron
The tower's clock frozen in time for 400 years
Now my only way by paths defined by stake and tape

The snoring, sleeping early morning homeless
Who used to shelter in the church's vaulted porches
Pushed out of Hackney to disinfected hotels,
Wake bewildered to breakfasts of dry toast
Covid cleansed onto strange streets
Risk must be kept away from the latte chatterati

In the Narrow Way the pound shop closed for bargains
No butchers or bakers or Covid mask makers
Instead, two metre blue pavement markings
Snake round the food bank queue
Gives the illusion of protection from infection
To poor people forced to queue to survive

The Law Centre is empty, but works off site, on-line
To stop an elderly disabled woman being evicted
To help a child from Calais woods join his brother here
To reverse wrong sanctioning from benefit
To stop time ticking, life slipping away
In our frightened world of C19.

I want to be a Lawyer Mam

I want to be a Lawyer Mam,
I'll be a Lawyer Dad.
I'll make you proud, I'll drive you round,
And take you both to town.

You can tell the neighbours Mam,
And the bowls team Dad.
Tell them all I worked so hard,
Now I'm off to Cardiff bound.

I won't forget my roots though Mam,
I'll remember, promise, Dad.
I'll speak for them that have no voice,
And make you both so proud.

Don't come to the office, Mam,
Don't buy me dinner Dad.
The office damp it breaks your heart,
This isn't the dream you had.

Oh I've had offers plenty, Mam,
But I won't take them Dad.
Though the fees are cut, we won't give up,
But the times is always hard.

There's children going hungry Mam,
And I can help them Dad.
And not just me, there's more you see –
Dotted through the land.

Cos Legal Aid I am now Mam,
A Law Centre Lawyer, Dad.
The girl from Swansea Town, now Bristol bound,
I hope I made you proud.

Skype hearing at ten, Zoom conference at two

Another day dawns and oh what to do,
Skype hearing at ten, Zoom conference at two.
And what does Mum have (cos we're home-schooling two)?
Zoom conference at ten, Skype hearing at two.

So where will we go to complete all these tasks?
The wife in the bedroom? Me in the bath?
Our backgrounds? No bookcase - we don't have the room.
A plain wall for Skype and the 'palm trees' for Zoom.

We're trying our best with the kids 'remote school'
The hardest of tasks is just keeping cool
My maths long forgotten - 'have you tried asking Mum?
She'll be in in a mo, when her hearing is done'.

The Court tech is struggling, judge going berserk,
(Remote criminal trials? Just not going to work).
Our 'world class justice system' would soon be a mess
Without all lockdown lawyers each doing our best.

Should we stay silent?

Should we stop
Holding those in power to account?
'They're doing their best...'
So our rights they can flout

Should we stay silent
Until the restrictions ease?
An unprecedented crisis
Means the government must do as they please

But what will come of society
when the pandemic comes to an end
If we are not there to question
And the most vulnerable we don't defend?

When what was 'necessary' becomes the new normal
and justice takes a back seat
Will we have a country we recognise?
Or will we watch the safeguards we are proud of deplete?

Or should human rights be front and centre
Of the response our government takes?
We must protect those who are most at risk
There couldn't be higher stakes

So we shall not be silenced
Our voices shall not be drowned
United for justice, together we stand
We will fight. We will stand our ground.

Remote

Today I had a hard day in (virtual) court.
My defendant got sent down.
That isn't anything new for a criminal barrister.

I was on Skype.
He was on unconditional bail.
His dad sat outside. Waiting.
'What about my dad?'

I wasn't there in person.
No one went down to see him.
It's been sunny in London and
I have a balcony to go to after the hearing.
It was his first custodial sentence.

Closed my laptop and walked away.
Sat in the sun and had a drink.
His dad sat outside.
Waiting.

My words.
My advocacy.
And then a decision handed down.

Mute.
And he was gone.

Drone pilot over a warzone.
And I'm back home.
My nice home.

Struggling to make it real.
Not traveling to court.
Not seeing, smelling, feeling him near me.
Now it's on a screen somewhere.

Reality.

Close your laptop and you'll forget all about it.

Remotely.

It was Corona Time in Kent

Spring wrapped itself in death this year.
Every snowdrop,
Every bud,
On every tree,
A memento mori.

The memory of your touch,
The colour of your eyes,
Once taken for granted,
Slip between the fingers
Of my outstretched hands.

Let us
Run to the woods,
You and I.

Let us
Throw ourselves on our backs
And stare at the sunlight-dappled leaves.

Let us
Hold hands once again, and listen
To the silence.

Silence.

Listen closer.
So silent,
You can hear
The bluebells ring.

The Future is Orange

I queued at the Aldi
To buy pasta and flour
But both those and Andrex
Were gone in an hour.

No loo roll or Dettol
No hand gel or eggs
No vaccines till Christmas
For those who aren't dead.

At first, I was worried
With no end in sight
But I turned on the TV
And see it's alright...

Forget all the scientists
Forget the EU
Forget personal responsibility
For the things that you do...

No need to stay separate
No need to stay in
Since president Trump says
Inject bleach for the win!

Footnote.
To the tune of 'On Top of Old Smokey'

Cooking

Overnight
It feels like the world
Has gone mad.
Unrecognisable
The smallest things
Taken for granted
Now a distant memory.
The fear is crippling.

I tell myself
That owning up to it
Will lessen its hold.
I make pastry
And try to be pleased
No soggy bottom here:
Something to celebrate!

The fragrances
Filling my kitchen
An attempt to recreate
My mother's food

She sends instructions
As I keep smiling.
Show her my face
Try to hide the worry.

My pride fights my fear:
Stay safe out there
Send your patients
Home to their families.

But my hero parents
I count the days
Until I can open your door
Pour you a drink
And raise our glasses
To you, to us
To family.

Criminal Defence Solicitor Blues

You never feel that special when you work in legal aid,
Unless relentless cuts are sexy and disrespect is what you crave.

Working day and night, weekends and each special holiday,
For a very low fixed fee, assumed by all to be good pay

It's much more like pro-bono, we do so much for free
The rate of pay it stays the same; we only get one fee.

We have to pay for audits, SQM's & peer reviews,
So the wages that we pay ourselves, they really don't enthuse

Now we are 'key workers' and still we are in Courts and
stations, with the public whom, they want us to consort

It's hard to socially distance in a room, two metres square
With three other people in it, plus police officers in pairs

There is no PPE for us, we must provide our own
but I couldn't find a mask or gloves lying around at home.

Still I went to that police station and I represented Fred
But Fred had COVID-19. And now me and Fred are DEAD

Spring 2020

I was trying to write about global agribusiness,
Capital and the destruction of habitats
Changing animal and biological behaviour,
These new margins the incubator of
Pandemics,
When my young son came and asked
If we could listen again
To the humming of the myriad wings
Of bees in the cherry blossom.

I put down my pen.

Footnotes

The era of pandemics is explained and predicted in the New Left Review 102, Nov/ Dec 2016, Wallace and Wallace, Agribusiness and the Ebola Virus.

The idea for this poem came from the great Bertolt Brecht poem Spring 1938.

Covid without my clerk

Inkjet printer woes
Two thousand pages to go
Black ink running low

Thoughts of this life in lockdown

It's all so uncertain,
When will it end?
This life in lockdown
Will it extend?

Overloading the Wi-Fi
Working from my room
Only getting dressed for
Meetings using Zoom

Some court hearings have stopped
Others take place online
The arrests seem to continue
With many a fine.

Waking up early to do the
Workout with Joe Wicks
But finding myself more tired
With the state of politics

Applauding all keyworkers
On a Thursday night
Makes me feel sadness
As I think of their plight.

This Covid pandemic
Has changed all our lives
We mourn the dead
And pray that the sick survive

C section

Section and C section
mania and motherhood,
I wonder at her resilience

The Isolation Blues

Ours is a profession of contradictions,
isolative but collegiate, wise but unhealthy,
threadbare poor but immensely wealthy,
apparently, we defend the guilty and
decry the victim's lot, no thought for truth
yet our word is our bond, a knot. Revered
and reviled in equal cuts, we fight for rights
that no-one wants, no government sustains us,
we remain the butt of jokes when axe and blade
are wielded to garner votes. And yet,
would we have it any other way?
Despite this travail, I really cannot say.

Still, it is the little things I miss,
the everyday insolence and obtuse
unpleasantness of security as they
open bags and humiliate advocates,
particularly women. 'What's this?'
peering at personal effects despite
the so-called protocols forbidding it.
A professional is worth their weight
in gold beside a jobsworth and so,
I make the point as seems fair. A recent
court where all the while a merry chat
and wry smile were met in kind each day.
Yes, the queues were slow, we had to wait
but simple cordiality and decency made
minutes fly, and so it did not grate.

I miss the foyer, you'll know the one,
redecorated in an elegantly characterless
swathe of lino whose colour sets my teeth
on edge. Discounting the lifts (broken again) I turn
to climb the steps and find, beyond the café

closed for years, the famous stairwell stain.
Whatever it may have been, and I'll not guess,
this mess remains a faithful friend. There,
on the landing bend, ingrained in mortar
since the '90s or before, it defies all decoration
or so called 'deep-clean'. The times I have
tripped up those stairs, and tripped upon
the loosened tread. Aah, happy days!
The memories leave me homesick for this place.

The stale airless space! Drab corridors, coffee
stained carpet squares, threadbare, with corners
turned sufficient to catch the unwary with a drink
but not to catch the eye of 'facilities' or
make them act or even think. I stroll slowly past
conference rooms locked against the risk of use
to sit in chairs so low that anyone of age or infirmity
has no prospect of standing without aid or abuse.
Oh, savour now the toilets on the second floor!
Unclean since time immemorial, whose slamming door
cracks the landing wall and floor. The unsightly damage
a work in progress these twenty years or more.

I long for the solemnity of the senior courts,
the panelling and leather in the great and old
whilst elsewhere, a wealth of exposed melamine,
ceilings gone to holes, some even falling down!
Seats angled to invoke sciatica
aggravated by the unheated cold,
whose dirty cloth now worn through
to screws artfully placed to rip a gown.
A bucket is welcome on the worst days but
wear your old clothes, not your best, and
in the winter you'll need a vest. Despite
the damage and the damp there is no heat,
nor anywhere now to eat. Long ago these courts
provided food of sorts and all could sup upon
some nameless dish, courting indigestion.

Was it meat or fish? Contracts awarded to the
cheapest fellow, it makes me weep, like a willow.

Did I say solemnity? Not in court four
whose resident bully from another age
would scream and rage at advocates for sport,
or worse. Thankfully his much-cursed perversity
has descended into isolation of a different sort.
Whilst some such characters remain
they are fewer now. Their loss is our gain.
Do I long for the dim hallway? The dirty windows
hidden behind nets whose nameless shade,
set somewhere between grey and filthy, illuminates
the stone floor. Polished in a nightly ritual
ancient and meaner than the old machine
swabbed to and fro by the cleaner. Alas that
such buildings linger, year on year, beyond old
as newer buildings are closed and sold.

I'll not speak of listing. There's little one can say
about a system that seems designed or run
to carry common sense away. Nor the MoJ
a cruel misnomer I bridle to see it writ or
hear it said. Don't mention the LAA! A quango
designed to ensure bankruptcy looms
at every stage of your career. Nor robing rooms,
nor cells infested with dead things, gloom and
protocols to keep logic at bay. Thank heaven
for those few warders who see the light of day,
for whom the rule book is not a creed! They
recognise the need for flexibility, to help, or
we'll be stuck here well beyond the close of day.
A little cooperation please! We all benefit from
avoiding a system that, left to its own devices
would have us on our knees!

I miss the inevitable kindness of the judge
in court six and in court nine. I owe them each

a debt of gratitude. I say so now on my part both
personal and professional. These gentle men
learned, respected and, yes, kind. They have
no point to prove nor axe to grind but listen
and bear in mind that justice and law
whilst both dispensed in this place
are not equal partners in every case.
In giving someone who has erred a chance,
tempering justice with mercy, they are
not the enemies of the people. Not deserving
of the gibes. Not the architects of legal woes
created by 'Failing' politicians bent on passing
blame who crow and strut in what seems
little better than a rut. They do not heed
the politician's call, to play with other
people's lives but seek to do fairness by all.

I miss the ushers! That mild band of folk ever helpful,
always ready, always there to share a joke, or
a handful of tissues when the water jug is broke.
They help bump someone up the list and smooth
the ruffled feathers of folk who wait. Their turn will come.
Some day they too will need a favour, and ushers,
with their slow gate (they rarely run) have memories
like elephants. No electronics can 'eXhibit' their skills.
Watch and learn, the power in the court may sit
on the bench but the usher is the engine!
Treat them fairly or it will go ill.

And while I'm on the subject of ills,
I'll not speak badly of the police.
They have a difficult job to do without resources.
Of course, we may not always see eye to eye,
I've seen errors, I've seen lies but that occurs
in all walks of life. Mostly I have seen
dedicated officers doing their best. And I say that
as someone who has both prosecuted and defended.
We have chatted and laughed, argued and fought

but I have seen real professionalism in many cases and,
been treated with courtesy when in court.

Some clients I miss. True they can be perverse
and some far worse but each has need of help.
Whether they deserve it, is not for me to say and
yes, I have defended someone I thought 'did it'.
But I have also defended (and prosecuted) some
I truly believed did not. It is no easy task to argue
for or against the incarceration of an innocent.
Some clients (and witnesses) are grateful for a chance
to have their say, some would spit and
never give you time of day. Perhaps that is the majority.
But there are occasions, few and far apart
when a thankyou is spoken quietly, from the heart
(I still recall a mum say,
'you have given me back my son.')
Despite the years, such moments still move me
to tears. And I would live it all again. The lack of pay,
the blows, the criticism, the ruined holidays,
the missed shows, the family pain,
the snide remarks from gutter press,
the early mornings and late nights to know
that I have done right, and, through me
someone has obtained freedom or redress.

Last but by no means least,
I miss the support of colleagues.
That brother and sisterhood of advocates
from firm and bar who greet old friends and
foes alike with gibes and kindly barbs.
Who joust in court with vim and zest,
whose word I trust! And, which is best,
I do so whether they are ally or adversary.
To work with or against a brief in total
confidence is remarkable indeed.
It provides relief, against the pressure
of missing something, taking a short cut,

the fear of being wrong (or right), the need
to work all hours of day and night. The loan
of a book, an authority, a wig or gown,
a quiet word, a pie and pint, a tenner
when the chips are down. In short, and this perhaps
is what these words stand for. I miss the Bar.

With all it's curious anachronisms, its flaws
its good and bad, its dark and light.
In upholding each other at whatever cost
we uphold justice and the law. Striving
as we may, to do what we believe is right.

C - Fever

I must go down to the courts again to the Royal Courts on the Strand
and all I ask is a dusty wig and a set of snow-white bands,
And a tough case that's worth the fight to set my heart a-racing,
And work all night to get it right by the grey dawn's breaking.

I must go down to the Temple lawns set by the river's tide
where the roses grow and the fountain sings by the old hall's side,
And all I ask is a moments peace to walk within the Inn,
to leave the legal day behind 'till the damn phone rings.

I must go down to the Old Bailey to fight for a poor man's life
To the wicked ways of drugs and guns and a fight with a whetted knife,
And all I ask is a fair trial although a man is dead,
As the door clangs and lies are told and justice hangs by a thread.

I must stand once more before the court and bid a fond farewell
To the brief's way and the bar's way, to where? I cannot tell,
And all I ask is a legal yarn from a fellow learned friend
A comfy seat and a quiet pint at the long day's end.

(With apologies to John Masefield)

Haiku

Imprisoned by Skype
Half-dressed jocularity
Invoicing dwindles

On the days gone by

On the days gone by, sometime in my past driving through a tunnel,
I broke down during the night.
A very cold, scary and dark night.
It felt like the end but I survived ...

This time around,
it feels like a breeze,
because I have built immunity to last me a lifetime.

I know I will be just fine.
Corona is a virus and I am a fighter.
I shall beat the opponent with spirit and a smile.

Covid saved my life tonight

(with thanks to Bernie Taupin & Elton John)

Covid saved my life tonight sugar bear
Crime almost had your hooks in me didn't you dear
You nearly had me roped and tied
Court bound, hypnotised
Covid freedom whispered in my ear
Fly away, high away, bye bye.

I always realised the passing hours of
evenings and weekends
A slip noose hanging in the darkest dreams
Strangled by Courts' haunting scenes
Just a pawn out played by a domain queen
It's four o'clock in the morning
Dammit Judge listen to me good
I'm not sleeping with myself tonight,
up to get the work done
Saved in time, thank God I'm still alive
Covid saved my life tonight sugar bear

And I might have walked head on into
the deep end of the river
Clinging to your indictment and exhibits
Paying your time demands forever
Then the world stopped, allowed me to catch up
But sweet freedom made me an outlier again; shame
Whisper it 'cos they'll come for you if they hear it
That whilst so many are suffering you found yourself
Dare not admit it, but I think
Covid might just have saved my life
Covid saved my life tonight, Covid saved my life tonight.

Undaunted Justice

We're a group who work (or will) in legal aid
It's tough, it's raw, it's badly paid
But we're not in it for the money
(Though junior pay cheques are quite funny).

We fight to keep the rule of law
But access to legal advice is poor
And so, the mandate of our fight:
Fund legal help, fund human rights.

We may be young, but we're not daunted
We'll help our members feel supported
And despite this current Covid crisis,
Know this our clients, we stand for justice.

Lockdown

The virus came; it will not go
Will we have trials by video?
The judge in chambers sits at home
Hearing pleas by telephone;
The advocates are dialling in,
The braver sort with tots of gin;
Discreetly placed, well out of sight
And praying they will not get tight.
They need support; does no one care?
Their incomes slashed; their futures bare.
Their human rights mean little now
Just pay your rent! For God's sake how?
The backlog grows; the system groans
Will I get tried? The client moans.
I'm stuck in jail; no chance of bail
Will Covid get me first? they rail.
No furloughed pay for m' learned friends
Will they survive?
The gloom descends;
No fees, no work, no legal aid
No clients to see, be not afraid;
The peak has passed, the curve has flattened
All depends on Chancellor Buckland.
He knows the score; knows what to do,
Open the courts, reduce the queue.
If he don't, the system crashes
The golden thread reduced to ashes.
No darkened courts; please hear our call
Let justice prevail, though the heavens fall.

Living My Best Lockdown Life

Not a difficult decision, to work from home or not
Claw back hours lost to travelling, and de-stress, a lot!
Setting a new routine, trying to keep things stable
Family become your new colleagues around
the dining room table
We're happy to stay home, save lives, protect the NHS
But it seems these days we see outside less and less

This whole new world of virtual meetings
keeps you all connected
Whoever heard of Zoom before late March,
had it even been invented?
Lockdown haircut horrors
on view during daily team meetings
And home office envy whilst we all exchange greetings
This new way of working meaning
you actually 'socialise' more
No excuses not to turn up,
like you might have made before

So as the weeks maybe turn to months,
and more time spent in lockdown
I think of the things we're missing, and this elicits a frown
But I must remember that at home we're protected,
And all our efforts and the time we've invested
Must not go to waste whilst we hanker for release
Even if it means I miss my holiday in Greece!

Easements

It's hard to breathe.
To believe
We're all in this together

The Secretary's daughter can get a test
But for the rest
Just stay home, hope for the best.

And if you're part of the amorphous 'BAME'
You know the sound
Of that familiar blame game

If you're Black
It's the lack
Of vitamin D

But you know, to me
That's no explanation
For institutionalised discrimination.

Remember us
Who get our care in the community.
You know the ones
First left
To herd immunity.

It can be difficult to see the light
At the end of the tunnel
When your access to care is barely a human right

We have to funnel it to those most in need
We're sorry for the fuss

But to me, barely able to make the tea
When they said ease
They meant for them and not with the likes of us.

With LJ
28 April 2020

Seeking

Want to work hard
... Got to feed kids

Want to help people
... Got to stroke cat

Must make a difference
... Got to get dressed?

Zoom screen is calling
To do list grows longer
My papers, kids' papers, merge into one

Access to justice. Precious and vital.
Me? One of the lucky ones.

Lucky

Seeking justice while
Inequality widens
Poverty deepens,
Horror.

Seeking solitude while
Working at home.
Sense of self,
Wobbles.

Fear and Loathing in the Time of Coronavirus

Roses are red
Violets are blue
Many courts are closed
And soon we will be too

Untitled

These cities do sleep
with unhappy children
as winter subsides

Say goodbye to your friends
try and recollect the last time
you looked into their eyes

Nowhere to go and
nowhere to hide when faced with
Earths ghastly surprise

Quarantine Dreams

Quarantine Dreams
They echo of you
Lament for a world
That I once knew

My salvation in song
For the facts are cryptic
I hope that my life
Will not be a statistic

We think that the world
Shall return soon after
But this is one stepping-stone
In a great disaster

Eerie normality shall rain
On our denatured lives
As we can only pray
The human spirit survives

Our lives we assumed solid
On the edge of absurd
Out from the dark ages
Ominous and unheard

A plague like virus
Has us out of our heads
Vanished from the west we thought
Now look at the dead

My Corona Quandry

As I drive to my office on my daily commute,
I pass the shutdown cafes, bars and shops.

The roads and pavements are empty,
as quiet as Christmas Day, even though it's not.

I do my virtual hearing, is that my opponent's bedroom?
Too late, the link has broken, back to my perpetual boredom.

Time for positivity, everything will reopen,
the deadly virus will be beaten and
we will return to real court rooms!

Bin Day

Every day is on repeat,
But none are the same as I look at my feet,
To fasten my shoes for a ride on the bike,
That is being used more than it would like.
The gears grind and the chain shudders,
The back wheel pulls to one side and feels like a rudder.
Escapism essential, I pedal as permitted,
No cars about, but MAMILS remain committed.
Every day is the same, except for bin day,
still circled on my calendar.

This day feels familiar without fail,
My inbox flows with electronic mail,
Things that were said now only exist when typed,
Including all those usual gripes!
My desk is where I used to eat,
Entering my 'office' with slippered feet.
A meeting conducted in joggers and a tee,
Feels a comfortable way to negotiate fees?
Another amnesiac day slips on by,
it's not bin day yet I say in my mind.

No prefix required on 'day' anymore,
I wake, I work, I eat, I snore.
'The court hasn't called me' Counsel cries out,
Indignant, exasperated, affronted, worn out.
Not much I can do, telegram the judge?
I am sure they will call – but justice does not budge!

This new normal is law from a comfy armchair,
No need to endure your opponent's hard stare.
But justice needs to be seen to be done,
and the bins need to be seen to be out.

On repeat now every day,
The radio wakes me and begins to say,
Here comes the news,
Explaining there are no liberties left to lose?
Losing time would be great,
Fast forward to that pint, with that mate.
The condensation slowly drips,
As I raise the glass to my lips...
Every day is the same, except for bin day,
still etched in my brain.

Twenty-four hours, the same as the last,
Six weeks along from our space invading past,
I hadn't noticed truth be told,
But it will hit me, and emotions unfold
When the bins next go out,
(More than you or I, no doubt).
Good on them, their outing well deserved,
And while I can still put them out,
I know I am preserved.

Clerking in Covid

I thought working in Chambers caused me stress,
And that now working from home it would cause me less.
But, have you ever tried explaining to a Barrister how to use Egress?

I always assumed remote hearings would take little time,
Although, to get it to work you need to be Einstein.
Re-explaining yet again how to use Zoom,
You didn't get any of this in the courtroom.

Counsel on the phone making a drama like it's Broadway
'You've got these already' is all I seem to say.
'It's one-minute past 10 and I haven't been dialled in'
'You're on the phone to me right now, how is it meant to begin?!'

It's all going well, then the WI-FI goes down,
I have a meeting in five minutes and still wearing my dressing gown.
Getting back ache from the dining room chair,
My neck hurts, brain frazzled and eyes going square.

I've almost forgotten what my work colleagues look like,
I wouldn't know now if they all went on strike!
Back in the good days, we'd all go to the pub
Now we do it via video like some weird night club.

Clerking from home does have a positive swing,
In my lunch hours I can now catch up with Tiger King.
Commute has reduced to five metres from my bed
Tesco meal deals no more, not when I can cook instead.
I'm now always in for deliveries to my door,
And I can wear comfier clothes than I could do before.
COVID-19 you've been a right royal pain,
I never thought I'd say it, but I'm looking forward to being
back in the office again!

Whizz Bang

Is that a whizz bang?
No
It's the delivery van
I'm not on the front line
I'm at home

I do what I'm told

I am told what to do so I do
If I don't keep away, I am shunned
Steer a wide berth so I do.
At the supermarket a select few
Shop like distant artists
No touching, no coming near
Lines to stand behind
Spots to wait on.
I am told what to do so I do
I mustn't see my parents, visit the care home,
go to the park, go to work or help others
I help others by doing what I am told
So I do
I mustn't complain
But I do!

2020

You started well
But then promise was dashed
February ushered in
The Year of the Rat

Never more than six feet away
So the urban legend goes,
March 2020
Better make that twelve

No showers in April
Bright sun, blossom, the Cuckoo
New life
New normal

Roll on May day
May day
Hope on hope
Our call will be heard

2020
The Year of the Rat
Damn right!

Quarantini

Stuck in my room,
A poor unfortunate tomb
Afraid and masked with fear,
Accompanied by beer.

When will it end?
If only amazon could send
A solution or a sign,
Or perhaps just more wine.

Soap and antibacterial
A Skype with Auntie Muriel
My patience has worn thin,
Time for a gin.

COVID-19
A virus I've never seen
Get inside, it's all too risky,
Open wide, have a whiskey.

Drunk in my room
Dancing with my broom
I've decided her name's Sheila,
Give me the tequila.

Long Holidays

Long holidays really aren't fun
On long holidays we can't go to school
Never go to thc dinosaur museum, but we do
Get outside and clap along!

Home is where we relax during long holidays,
Or work! Or exercise! Basically everything!
Long holidays really aren't fun ... !
I miss Miss Hunt during long holidays.

Do not go out! Except for one person.
A sunny day is so wonderful during long holidays.
Yesterday, today and tomorrow are all the same,
even school days.
School's out but I can't wait to get back!

Blaming Plants

Ever wondered.
What is under.
Your boot.
The maze in.
Our soil.
That starts with.
One root.
I watch my succulent.
Growing stronger.
Each day I water.
Each day it's longer.
If it stops growing.
I don't blame the plant.
I will start an.
Insufferable rant.
It must be the sun.
The room.
The soil.
The poor little plant.
No one meant.
To spoil.
And maybe I forgot.
To water each day.
But blaming the plant.
I would never say.
We are the plants.
The roots.
The maze.
We won.
And maybe we.
All need a bit more sun.

Not Forgotten

Darkness follows the passing of the light,
Emotions peaked to almost eternal night

We persevere our senses heighten,
Gradually the pressure starts to lighten

Pushing through and pressing strong
Where there was one, we are together, an increasing throng.

The devastation, the chaos, it passes
The level of sacrifice not forgotten by the masses

Coping with Covid

Confined to indoors when outside the weather is so fine
A bang on the door it's Waitrose with a delivery of wine
Hasty donning of plastic gloves spray sanitiser on the box
In my London street animals now roam, squirrel, cat, fox

First it was no loo rolls and stocking up of food
Then getting to know my family, and not all of that was good
Skype, Zoom and Lifesize have kept my practice at full steam
But I've also learnt to hoover, iron decorate and clean

Never before did I realise what my two dogs meant to me
Their affection a revelation despite a backyard full of pee
And my little garden for the first time being tended so well
A patch of green of sitting room size has become the holy grail

I have given up wondering what will happen after lockdown
Will the world be a nicer place or just a lot more overgrown?
And will the journalists and broadcasters stop talking down at us
Then simple joys will return, like travel by tube, train and bus

Will we forget the Thursday nights clapping on the step
Will we value human life with more humanity and depth
What will we feel when ambulance sirens cease to wail?
I hope and pray we'll show compassion for all and will not fail

'Very Strange Times'

There I was, cup of tea in hand,
Sat in my bed, with terrible broadband.

I was waiting for a call, from the court clerk,
The bin men pulled up, caused my dog to bark.

Finally, the court called, albeit two hours late,
And I sat in my PJs, ready to advocate.

Parents interrupting, wanting the last word,
Lawyers raising objections, unable to be heard.

Although this all sounds strange and bemusing,
In fact, it is clear that the justice system is losing.

The vital reassurances, that lawyers put in place,
Cannot be effective, when it isn't face-to-face.

In 'child removal hearings' parents are unable to connect,
Unable to fight those allegations of neglect.

Parents trying to listen, whilst children are running riot,
Wishing that they had a bit of peace and quiet.

It goes without saying, that these are very strange times,
Where the virus continues to ring, its melancholy chimes.

But the country will get through it, just you wait and see,
As long as we keep on smiling, I am sure you would agree.

Remote Justice

Legal aid lawyers will always fight the good fight

We will never give up when it comes to your rights

COVID-19 is making things tough

Lockdown is hard, its mentally rough

But we are all still here, the virus won't stop me

Fighting for justice, working remotely

Lucky to be here!

The disruption to our life
24/7 in a four-walled paradise
No more trials about who had the knife
But ... we're the lucky ones

No chambers, no court
No loo roll can be bought
Wherever you look, people are fraught
But ... we're the lucky ones

I've missed seeing the Masters
And more Arsenal disasters
Now my cricketing blasters
But after all ... we're the lucky ones

So, I've decided to decorate
To never be an ingrate
And stay up with Netflix till late
Cos so far so good ... we're the lucky ones!

We are six weeks in and nowhere to go
For some strange reason it doesn't seem slow
But unlike many, my hair still won't grow
Always thankful ... we're the lucky ones!

So what does lockdown bring?
Certainly life without bling,
Unless you are Joe Exotic ... the true Tiger King
But for me, just being here. Cos I am a lucky one!

Lockdown Poem

Could you write a lockdown poem, they asked?
Of course! I can tweet rubbish for England, me,
How hard can it be?
It's not like there's anything else to do
In this mundanely surreal time vortex
We call normal now. A poem? Easy!
How hard can it be?
Turns out it's not easy wrangling poems
Out of words when time has lost its structure.
How hard can it be?
Turns out it's not easy at all. It's hard.

I'll stay happy

When you carry.
A heavy load.
For longer.
It gets easier to bear.
I'm not saying.
I'm not gutted.
It's always there.
My shoulders are stronger.
Though my back will still ache.
But I'll stay happy.
For your sake.

Lament of a prohibited dog

I was seized because of my appearance
On the balance of probabilities I am a pit bull type.
My owner went to court before the need for skype
The court concluded that in their experience
I could be set free

The Court said I was not dangerous
My nature was friendly, and I was a loving pet.
So long as the conditions of the exemption were met
I could go home on mandatory conditions without a fuss
This was to be within two months

I am in secret kennels which seems like a holding centre
But they won't release me till I am spayed.
The veterinary surgeon however has delayed
Because of COVID-19 he will not enter
Time is passing I am still here

The Court said I am not a dangerous dog
We are trying to extend the time to save me.
I have done nothing wrong you see
But I fear now there is a backlog
I fear for my life

I don't know why I can't go home on conditions
And another vet do the surgery.
As my life is at stake there is some urgency
My owner will comply with all stipulations
Set out in the exemption scheme.

So this is where I am right now just because of my looks
I am simply a cross bred dog a mix of I don't know what.
If not exempted destruction is my lot
Many want this law changed to update the books
So it will be based only on deed and not on breed.

My owners are just distraught
They miss me and are constantly tearful.
They had no clue I was unlawful
So nobody nor I was at fault
Research shows I am no more a risk than any other.

My friend here in kennels has no owner
He was found in the street abandoned.
Because he is a stray, he is condemned
Lovely nature friendly a socialite not a loner
This discrimination is so unfair.

If not for the lock down I could be free,
If the vet would do the operation
It would ensure my emancipation.
The virus has kept me from liberty
Please give me a mask and PPE.

It's not going ahead

It started not too long ago
My clerks called me up and said
You know that hearing in your diary?
Turns out it's not going ahead.

The first time it happened
I wasn't in much of a fix.
More time to lie in, to snack;
And binge a new series on Netflix.

The second time it happened
The novelty still hadn't worn off
Better to sit at home on the sofa tucked up than
To venture out and come back with a worrying cough.

Then it happened a third time
And I was starting to get a bit irked.
The unexpected holiday was all good and well
But I couldn't remember the last time I'd worked.

I confess I'm now becoming resigned
To being a reluctant lady of leisure.
What I wouldn't give for just one hearing;
I'm even starting to miss the pressure.

I never thought I'd see the day
When with excitement instead of dread;
I'd happily go to the middle of nowhere,
Because my hearing is actually going ahead!

Stop All The Courts

Stop all the courts, switch us to telephone,
Prevent the dog from barking before dialling in,
Silence your microphone and, with muffled drum
Bring out the webcam. Let the video-link come.

Let counsel sit moaning that the audio is stilty
Scribbling on the Skype the message,
HE'LL PLEAD GUILTY
Put a suit jacket around our necks as we sit at our browsers
Let the judges think that we're still wearing trousers.

Attend the Circuits: North, South, East and West,
In the space of an hour, with no time to rest.
Billing ninety pounds a week, still working fifty hours strong.
I thought I might get financial assistance. I was wrong.

Our fees clerks are not wanted now,
Furlough every one.
Pack up our wigs and leave our collars undone,
Fold up our robes, light up a cigar, for nothing now but
Luck and lunch will save the Criminal Bar.

Gonna sit right down and write myself a brief

I'm gonna sit right down and write myself a brief
And make believe it came from you
I'm gonna read it with relief
It's gonna knock me off my feet
12 jury case tomorrow
I'll be glad am not in furlough

I'm gonna smile and say I hope you're feeling better
And email to say I'm on my way
With a wig and gown returned from the cleaner
And make believe for my sarnies it will pay

I'm gonna get my Archbold and laptop so they're ready
And make believe we don't need PPE
I'll take my ruler and check the safety
And space to see the client at liberty

I'm gonna sit right down and check the Digi system
And sign in to check it's not a dream
Gonna make believe there's legal aid
And travel and attendance in the scheme
With make believe there's PPE, I am not afraid

I'm gonna sit right down and write myself a skeleton
Setting out the submissions for you
And make believe they'll pass inspection
And make believe this is all so true

I'm gonna sit right down and smile to say there's justice
Gonna make believe we've seen this through
and unless the protocol applied with conscientiousness
Gonna make believe there's been no interview
Gonna make believe the custody is suite
Gonna make believe all are safe.

Legal Luckdown

A peculiar condition has descended on my street
Where everyone is staying in, and putting up their feet
They say it's down to sneezing, and a bat in deepest China
And all-inclusive tourists cruising home upon a liner

No work, no pay, the courts are shut, be sure to stay away
No work, no pay, your case is out, the same again today

Now pigeons sit in judgment on my court of plastic grass
Where sunny days are wiled away, reclining on my arse
I'm mindful of my mental health, cue Joe for morning training
How we crunched and bunny-hopped, until it started raining

The world is on a furlough, or that's the way it seems
And four-fifths of their salary feels like the stuff of dreams
But even so could they just have five minutes of my day
To solve these little issues that have troubled them today

So, on the kitchen table, all toast and football stickers,
The emails gush from legal types, home working in their knickers
The bedroom needs arranging sharp, to clear a space to type
I comb my hair and splash my face to brush up nice for Skype

No work, no pay, the courts are shut, be sure to stay away
No work, no pay, you've got no trial, the same again today

The kids are all in rapture, they say school is out for summer
But will a thousand worksheets really stop them getting dumber?
Please make them do their homework, and tidy up their socks
Given half a chance I'd take a hammer to X-Box

Super-parents post away, their feats of derring-do
With children reading Shakespeare whilst they're sitting on the loo
Or they climb the Eiffel Tower whilst just running on the spot
'Cos super-kids are such a big improvement on your lot

Who fight and scream and fight again, divided by a wall
From grouchy neighbour's flower beds, all flattened by their ball
We haul them off around the park, all parted by two metres
While special cops patrol the scene to apprehend the cheaters

No work, no pay, perhaps July, but surely in September
Far too late to save the scraps of law that I remember

My prison breaks out once a week to clap and cheer our nurses
(None of which is any help improving on my verses).
The locals seem contented, they say it fits their style,
'Perhaps a mortgage holiday might suit you for a while?'

How goes it at the hospital? I hardly dare to ask
We're cutting up our curtains to use them as a mask
The Docs have been heroic and curve is past its peak
They'll soon be testing everyone, in just a few more weeks

The talk is all about the plan to justify some easing
When might we pop out to the pub? That would be very pleasing
The government say they're there for us, to steer us to the end
But will come in time to stop me going 'round the bend?

No work, no pay, the bills are in, it's looking pretty bleak
No work, no pay, and on it goes, the same again next week

Lost In Digitisation

People are scared these days
Unable to manage their fears
For many it's not a new feeling
They've felt powerless for years

It is rare someone goes to court on a whim
Most discussions are best placed elsewhere
But without sufficient advice and support
No one explains what is fair and not fair

People should have their cases heard
No one deserves any less
Lockdown gives safety to flatten the curve
And precious data for HMCTS

Judges can preside over virtual court rooms
Covering vast distance with their (imaginary) gavel
'The benefits are endless, clients will love it
Savings on waiting times/security/travel!'

Government will cite the profession's quick response
Wigged and gowned up in their houses
Hoping there won't be an appearance
From any rogue dogs, children or spouses

Yet clients might have a different view
If they are online at all
Unheard, unseen, not participating
Not just their image feeling ignored and small

Do any lawyers think this is ideal?
Hunched up like surly teenagers on instant chat
Connections poor you hear other word
All parties require a better service than that

It is important to remember the clients
Remain central in all this noise
Doing our best for now is not best for the future
Before courts close and budget managers rejoice

Courts are the one place, in theory
Where you're looked in the eyes and right is done
If justice becomes remote and this is not standard
It is a loss for lawyers, clients, everyone.

Lost in thought

Lockdown lawyer lost in thought
Thinking of clients
Past, present and those to come
Clients with health conditions
I hope they are well
Victims of domestic violence
Let them be safe
Homeless families
Make sure they are suitably housed
Are they okay and how will they cope?
When this is over, will it be over for them?
Legal aid lawyer lost in thought

Bail in a Time of Coronavirus HC/99800

The hearing is by phone
And the clerk calls in advance
The lawyer is at home
Where he's sitting in his pants

The client's in an IRC
Where hundreds still are stuck
A place that wasn't all that swish
Before the virus struck

The circumstances of the case
Recall the Twilight Zone
There's no remote instructions
When your client has no phone

The reasons for opposing bail
Would make a lawyer nervous
To say they're largely bollocks
Would do testicles disservice

Here's a man who's dangerous:
To give you some idea
He's had several parking fines
And went the wrong way round IKEA

He's hell-bent on remaining
And will by hook or crook,
He waddled out of Harmondsworth
While dressed up as a duck

It took 15 men from Serco
To detain and drag him back
Wasted several hours and
He couldn't give a quack

It doesn't take a genius
To guess this isn't true
But without instructions
There is nothing you can do

On prospects of removal
The Home Office is vague
Telling by its absence
Is a reference to the plague

The Judge appears upon the line
The lawyer is subdued
(It's often hard to concentrate
When speaking in the nude)

So right – hmmm! – this young man -
Removal's in the offing?
(The Home Office's rep
Has a sudden fit of coughing)

Sorry – what – ahem!
Are they coming with the shackles?
(The Home Office's line
Now suspiciously just crackles)

Removal then is imminent?
Within a reasonable time?
(If the rep is speaking
Then the medium is mime)

I take it from your silence
That there's not a chance in hell
I'm letting this man out
And the next one out as well.

The hearing is a pantomime
It's all a pointless fudge
So, if a man absconds
Then the press can blame a judge

'Detainees get all they need'
Is the official statement
The intention may be there
But the content's Priti vacant

At least the client's out and free
To roam beneath the skies
As long as it's just briefly
In the course of exercise

The barrister hangs up the phone
And closes down his browsers
It's amazing what a lawyer
Can achieve without his trousers.

In the Arms of my Justice

Objection your honour!
her voice cries ‘round the rafters
for the coffee’s run out
Leave it love, that chocolate’s for afters.

Away from The Big Smoke, up in my attic:
far from the tube
tuned out from the static.
Lady Justice awaits,
with blindfold and scales.
To break bottle for voyage,
winds catch in her sails.

When our coughs turn to splutters,
tight blue ties start to stutter
‘Batten down the hatches
Board up the shutters’

Prime-time Beeb and the like,
may pitch Union Jacks in the dike.
But 5pm and the billboards
won’t stop it coming up through the floorboards.

Hammer our hands, wrought unto iron
un-count the change and block out the sirens.
Forget the duchess, lay down that old cutlass.
Seek benefit, build buttress:
In the arms of my Justice.

Click clack the keys atop the board,
to turn our compass north to ward
away the winds that stopped your vessel.
Foot off the pedal and stick on the kettle.

To the lost and found, neglected and spurned
'not today' they said, 'the court's adjourned'.
Lay down your musket, come out from the rushes:
Find space to lay, rest in the arms of my Justice.

Above doom and gloom
the storm roars asunder.
Idly embers spark forth,
and ashen thine plunder.

The bells are a-chiming
the flowers do bloom.
It's time to dial in,
she calls it a 'Zoom'.

But like Adam and Eve,
modest through apple and fig.
I know those are jimjams,
under that red robe and grey wig.

I would rather

I can't see any hate.
Only tenderness.
And love.
From the nurses.
From the doctors.
When push comes to shove.
If I have to leave.
My family.
In the care of.
Someone else.
I would rather it be you.
If it couldn't be myself.